LIFE'S TOO SHORT
Not To Do Crazy Stuff

PATRICK WALLER

Patrick Waller
Lifestyle Financial Planner

Patrick entered the financial services industry in 1979, working for Prudential. Dissatisfied with the restrictions of a single provider Patrick decided he wanted to offer independent financial advice, so he left the Pru to set up his own firm and in 1985 Financial Planning Partners was born.

From the outset, Patrick's mission has always been to deliver the highest quality financial planning advice backed with the best technical knowledge, experience, training and the ability to apply those qualities in order to have a positive impact on the lives of FPP's clients.

His insistence on the highest technical standards means that Patrick holds the coveted Chartered Financial Planner status (APFS) awarded by the Personal Finance Society. He also holds advanced qualifications in Pensions, Investment Planning, Taxation, Trusts and Investment Portfolio Management as well as additional qualifications in mortgages, equity release, and case study analysis. He is a member of the Chartered Insurance Institute and complies with their Code of Conduct and Ethics.

Patrick is keen on keeping fit, and is the 40th person in the world to have completed the Marathon Grand Slam which involves running a marathon on all 7 continents as well as at the North

Pole. In November 2013, he also ran marathons in the Antarctic and Chile with his daughter Charlotte, making them the third father/daughter marathon running team in the world to have run marathons together on all 7 continents.

Patrick is a keen supporter of local charities having raised over £5,000 for DEBRA. For his two marathons runs in the Antarctic and Chile in November 2013 he raised over £3,000 for Daisy's Dream, a charity devoted to supporting children and their families affected by both life threatening illness and bereavement throughout Berkshire and surrounding areas.

These days the marketing folk would have us believe that there is always a firm, person, provider or investment philosophy that is "the best" or "unique" or "new". Something extra special that provides the holy grail of investing, saving tax, or providing a service, and yet very often, when you "climb under the bonnet" there is little that is new or unique.

At FPP, We don't think that people are that gullible. It's a bit like saying that a BMW is way better than a Mercedes, or a Ferrari is way better than a Lamborghini. The reality is that they are all fine cars but just do things slightly differently or more flamboyantly. Some people prefer BMWs, some Mercedes, some Audis, some Jaguars.

And some prefer Ferraris... but they tend to be expensive to run, can go wrong big time and cost plenty of money to fix. This analogy can be a fair reflection of many investment strategies that are said to be "new", "unique" or "market beating"; those that promise the holy grail of investing, i.e. high returns with low risk. We often see such investment offerings "go wrong" and then, inevitably, costing money to fix.

To take the car analogy further, what IS important and relevant is that a modern car is faster, quieter, safer, cheaper to insure, more economical and built to last. Financial advice has developed in a similar way.

There are indeed cutting edge technologies and financial, investment and tax solutions that we employ in order to be able to deliver first class solutions to our clients in a cost efficient manner. Both these solutions and our firm are built to last and in the process deliver a first-class ownership experience.

We acknowledge that there are some excellent financial planners out there with great skill and expertise. By the same token we are proud to count ourselves amongst some of the best around; one of only 500 or so Chartered Financial Planning firms out of a total of around 16,000 financial planning practises. Sometimes the bits of paper count for something, and sometimes not - we think our chartered status begins to paint a picture of a professional firm dedicated to excellence.

We notice that many firms and advisers make a point of trotting out a list of adjectives describing qualities such as "integrity", "trust", "outstanding technical expertise", "product knowledge", "wealth management expertise" as though these are qualities that are new or unique… or in some way *optional*.

We think that's a bit odd. We believe that these qualities should be taken as read. They should never be in doubt and should be a starting point and not a value added extra. For FPP these qualities form part of the culture of the firm and always have done, which is why the business continues to thrive after almost 30 years.

Financial Planning Partners Ltd
19 Wellington Business Park
Dukes Ride, Crowthorne
Berkshire   RG45 6LS

Tel: 01344 778 990

www.fpp-ifa.co.uk

CONTENTS

"Actually I have no regard for money. Apart from its purchasing power, it's totally useless as far as I am concerned."

ALFRED HITCHCOCK

Introduction: **Life's Too Short**

The world of finance is often seen as murky and shrouded in mystery. Words like "efficient frontier", "earnings price ratio", "yield", "total return", "spread"... are often enough to send the investing public running for the hills. All too often they just want someone to take away the perceived pain of investing, cut through the gobbledegook and just invest the money for them.

In my experience people want an adviser they can trust implicitly. They are happy to pay a fair day's pay for a fair day's work, someone who is expert technically and will make sure that their plans are fulfilled and will look after them.

That's fine and there are many good advisers out there, but

in my view there is a catch; investing money at its very core is relatively simple. There are basic rules that immovable and, if followed, will provide the best possible outcome.

But it's not just about the money. It's about living the life you want to live without worrying about money, whether that be retiring early, giving money to children to help them buy their first home, going on the world cruise, buying the Aston Martin - **all before it's too late.**

This book is about something I am passionate about – life. Not just waking up in the morning and doing the everyday stuff. It's about living life to the full and using money for its intended purpose. It's about money being a means to an end and not the end in itself, as an instrument of pleasure and not an instrument of torture. For me, life is for living and I have seen way too many people die or succumb to illness without having experienced life to the full. It's about waking up to the inevitable fact that we are here but for the blink of an eye. It's about NOT being the wealthiest man/woman in the graveyard. It IS about lying on your deathbed with 24 hours left to live, with a big and very mischievous grin on your face, while you giggle to yourself whispering "that was so much fun". Yes, you'll be sad to leave your loved ones behind but happy that you spent so much quality time with them. This book is about how to do it. It's about the rules of investing and it's about making it all happen - all the secrets you need to know. **The stuff the "system" would rather you didn't know about.**

Ultimately money is pretty boring. Once you cut through the hype, or the "financial porn", that bombards us and the poor hapless investor trying to plan his future it's actually quite simple. Yep, I promise you, the principles are simple and it's actually relatively easy to make money out of the stock market provided you stick to certain principles and don't become stupid or seduced.

In this book, I'll give you some tips for making a real and lasting difference to your finances and to make you money. Sometimes it is about saving money, which is exactly the same as making money. It's about you keeping your returns, and not paying someone to gamble with your money and then ask you to pay through the nose for it.

It's about the secrets of the investment industry and also some secrets of the marketing industry. It's about how to wake up to the ways in which people (and more frequently institutions) make money out of you - and how to use the system to make money.

It is NOT about any kind of get rich quick scheme. Get rich quick schemes are usually just that – schemes. The only slight problem is that usually it is not you who will get rich quick; it is usually someone else at your expense. (With these schemes you will usually "Get Poor Quick"!) The old adage "if it's too good to be true, it almost certainly is" is well worn but quite frankly, all you need to know. By the time you realise it's a scam it's too late. Don't do it and avoid at all costs.

The chapters in this book won't be long and there won't be lengthy explanations. There will be more than enough information for you to figure it all out and to start to make sound investment decisions based on knowledge and to know how to create a plan and then execute it. Or of course you can pay someone else to do it and get on with enjoying life… yep – that's a plug. However I promise it's the only one.

"Twenty years from now you will be more disappointed by the things you didn't do than by the ones you did do.

MARK TWAIN

Chapter One: **Why Me? Why Now?**

We all know it. We hear it. We even pretend to understand the concept. But how many actually live it? We watch TV programmes about cool/crazy/brave people doing stuff that we would never dream we could do and so we get stuck. We get stuck in the "if, when, then" paradigm. When I have enough money, when I have more time, when the kids grow up. When I have had more time to think about it, to plan it, and then execute whatever plan I have in mind. These are known as "excuses".

We procrastinate, seek the opinion of others, have committee meetings, prepare clever presentations and somehow the magic doesn't happen. The dream remains a dream. In the words of Pink Floyd in the track "Time":

Ticking away the moments that make up a dull day
You fritter and waste the hours in an offhand way.
Kicking around on a piece of ground in your home town
Waiting for someone or something to show you the way.

Tired of lying in the sunshine staying home to watch the rain.
You are young and life is long and there is time to kill today.
And then one day you find ten years have got behind you.
No one told you when to run, you missed the starting gun.

So you run and you run to catch up with the sun but it's sinking
Racing around to come up behind you again.
The sun is the same in a relative way but you're older,
Shorter of breath and one day closer to death.

Every year is getting shorter never seem to find the time.
Plans that either come to naught or half a page of scribbled lines
Hanging on in quiet desperation is the English way
The time is gone, the song is over,
Thought I'd something more to say.

If you are around the same age as me you can sing along to that one in your head. And do you know what, if you can then please remember that *Time* was written in 1973, meaning the album from which it was taken was at the top of the chart forty-one years ago.

So take a moment to think; that was forty-one years ago. Are you where you wanted to be in your life? Have you done all those things you set out to do? Have you spent as much time with your children as you wanted to? Your friends?

"Much work is merely a way to make money; much leisure is merely a way to spend it.

C WRIGHT MILLS

CASE STUDY ONE: Sienna

This is the true story of one of my clients. Let's call her Sienna.

Sienna is married to James. They have no children but that's fine. They had planned their retirement meticulously taking full advantage of all the tax breaks available such as pensions, ISA/TOISAs/PEPs/NISAs/ISAs. (We think the government should launch a savings account called BLPA – Bucket List Provision Account). They have lived well but relatively modestly but have never denied themselves a great standard of living.

However they have both worked hard, in particular Sienna - working long, long hours for one of the major UK accountancy firms.

Way back in 2009 I did the maths for them and said, in no uncertain terms "look, based on your current assets, income and spending plans you have more than enough money to retire straight away. Now, not 2016 (as planned)".

I did my best to persuade them to hang up their boots and have fun.

But that's up to them. Being cautious bunnies they decided to carry on working, just in case they ran out of money (which every by the most cautious assumptions was impossible because so much of their retirement income was guaranteed).

And then it happened.

Around a year ago. It was a Monday morning and I remember it like it was yesterday.

I got an email from Sienna. She had just been diagnosed with oesophageal cancer. As it was pretty aggressive she started chemo and radiotherapy straight away.

Now, a year or so later she is better but her life expectancy is around 5 years or so, maybe more. However she has lost loads of weight and is much weaker than before and gets tired easily.

Sienna and James love walking holidays, now Sienna's illness limits them to shorter, more gentle trips. The Inca trail might be off the agenda which is so sad as walking this trail was on their list. I've walked the Inca trail and it's fabulous.

This is TRAGIC, and a waste. It does my head in. It makes me sad and as I write, emotional. Hence the title of this book.

If you have enough money CARPE DIEM!

If you love your work that's great, but remember the things you could have done and wanted to do.

In the words of Pink Floyd:

"And then one day you find ten years have got behind you. No one told you when to run, you missed the starting gun. So you run and you run to catch up with the sun but it's sinking".

Don't do it.

"Investing should be
more like watching paint dry or
watching grass grow.
If you want excitement, take
$800 and go to Las Vegas."

PAUL SAMUELSON

Chapter Two: **How Can the System Be Used to Make You Money?**

Think about great financial planning as a regret prevention service. If you stick to some basic principles and rules, you will make money. If you really must have a go at making a quick buck out of trading individual shares (we can't be bothered – too time consuming and tedious) then there are ways to trade stocks and shares that you can use to make money relatively predictably. We tell you which websites and trading methods to use. After that you are on your own. If you really MUST try it, then make sure it's with money that you can absolutely definitely afford to lose.

We will not cover any kind of geared trading such as Contracts for Difference (we call them Contracts for Disaster), options such as puts, calls and all that stuff. It's outside the scope of this book and not what we are about. You must remember that risk and reward are inextricably linked. I will share with you one of many ways of trading stocks and shares that you can take away and use to make money. It will however take time, effort and perseverance on your part. You may enjoy it or you may not. In my day job as a financial planner it is not something I get involved in - life's too short. You need to go and do it yourself. We give you actual methods, website addresses and trading information that you can use to give it a go but be prepared to lose the money you "invest".

We don't do it ourselves, as we can't be bothered. It's too much like hard work and we like to make money in predictable ways using the principles that we know work.

Chapter Three: **The Four Main Factors Driving the Stock Market**

Fear; Greed; Supply and Demand

There is an old saying on Wall Street that the market is driven by just two emotions: fear and greed. Although this is an oversimplification, it can often be true. Succumbing to these emotions can have a profound and detrimental effect on investors' portfolios and the stock market. The same goes for supply and demand.

Greed's Influence

Very often, investors get caught up in greed, also known as excessive desire. After all, most of us have a desire to acquire as much wealth as possible in the shortest amount of time.

The internet boom of the late 1990s is a perfect example.

At the time it seemed all an advisor had to do was simply pitch any investment with a ".com" at the end of it, and investors leapt at the opportunity. Buying activity in internet-related stocks, many just start-ups, reached a fever pitch. Investors got greedy, fuelling further greed and leading to securities being grossly overpriced, which created a bubble. It burst in mid-2000 and kept leading indexes depressed through 2001.

This get-rich-quick mentality makes it hard to maintain gains and keep to a strict investment plan over the long term especially amid such a frenzy, or as the former Federal Reserve chairman, Alan Greenspan, put it, the "irrational exuberance" of the overall market.

It's times like these when it is crucial to maintain an even keel and stick to the basic fundamentals of investing, such as maintaining a long-term horizon and avoiding getting swept up in the latest craze.

We would be remiss if we discussed the topic of not getting caught up in the latest craze without mentioning a very successful investor who stuck to his strategy and profited greatly. Warren Buffett showed us just how important and beneficial it is to stick to a plan in times like the dotcom boom; Buffett was once heavily criticized for refusing to invest in high-flying tech stocks - but once the tech bubble burst, his critics were silenced. Buffett stuck with his comfort zone: his long-term plan and by avoiding the dominant market emotion of the time - greed - he was able to avoid the losses felt by those hit by the bust.

Fear's Influence

Just as the market can become overwhelmed with greed, the same can happen with fear ("an unpleasant, often strong emotion, of anticipation or awareness of danger"). When stocks suffer large losses for a sustained period, the overall market can become more fearful of sustaining further losses. But being too fearful can be just as costly as being too greedy.

Just as greed dominated the market during the dotcom boom, the same can be said of the prevalence of fear following its bust. In a bid to stem their losses, investors quickly moved out of the equity (stock) markets in search of less risky buys. Money poured into money market securities, stable value funds and principal-protected funds - all low-risk and low-return securities.

This mass exodus out of the stock market shows a complete disregard for a long-term investing plan based on fundamentals. Investors threw their plans out the window because they were scared and overrun by a fear of sustaining further losses. Granted, losing a large portion of your equity portfolio's worth is a tough pill to swallow, but even harder to digest is the thought that the new instruments that initially received the inflows have very little chance of ever rebuilding that wealth. Just as scrapping your investment plan to hop on the latest get-rich-quick investment can tear a large hole in your portfolio, so too can getting swept up in the prevailing fear of the overall market by switching to low-risk, low-return investments at precisely the wrong time. That's called "being stupid". The antidote is simple - for which do not read "easy".

Stick to sound investment decisions while controlling your

emotions, whether it be greed or fear, or the effects of supply and demand. Create a sound long term investment strategy and stick to it. If you see that the stock market has crashed on the 6 o'clock news, switch channels and watch "The Simpsons". That'll be a better use of your time and more fun. It'll take your mind off the nonsense and the noise and by then it's too late anyway. If you sell out then, you make absolutely sure that you lose the game. For everyone who sells, there is a buyer. What do you suppose those buyers are looking for? Yep, people like you who sell out cheaply. Don't do it.

What is the antidote?

Be **honest** with yourself when you make your investments and how you can cope with the risks associated with those investments. Enlist someone who knows you well to explore your attitude to risk in detail. When you think about risk and the fact that you may well lose money (on paper at least) get real - to hell with logic, how will you REALLY feel? Ask your significant other or someone who knows you well to work through it with you. Emotion and logic are different animals.

As an exercise, prepare a dummy investment portfolio statement and then put a big fat minus next to the "portfolio value change since last year" and then really get in to how that would feel. If you will be scared, then tone down the risk profile you have selected. You may even be better keeping your money in a bank and making sure you just have more of the stuff to start with.

To hell with what other people think and the statistics: **YOU** are the most important person here. It's your money; your hard earned cash and you **MUST** invest in the way that suits you. Whilst you mustn't forget the well-worn warnings around investing in cash (primarily that you will usually lose money due to the effects of inflation) you may be happy to accept that risk in return for your own peace of mind.

Then if you have created a sound plan, based on the fundamental principles in this book, and the market does crash, don't buy in to the emotion. Switch channels if you're watching it on television, do the Sudoku puzzle if you are reading the paper, go for a walk, but do NOT react and sell. That is the way of fools. All you will do is line the pockets of those preying on your stupidity.

The next aspect is to not expect what you don't inspect. Find out how much you really spend each month and not how much you think you spend each month. Think very carefully about how much you will want to spend in retirement (if that's your goal) and then plan around that. For example, don't think along the lines of "I'd be quite happy to downsize my house to release cash" when you know damn well that you really love your home and wild horses will never drag you out of the front door. Create a budget and find out how much you REALLY spend.

CASE STUDY TWO: Giles & Angie

This is about Giles (not his real name but I think the name Giles is cool) and Angie.

I started my business many years ago on the 5th October 1985. Giles was my very first client. I arranged his first mortgage whilst he still lived with his Mum. He met Angie, fell in love and they got married. They had two wonderful daughters, Natalie and Emily who are happy and well on their own way in life.

Giles worked for an airline where he loved working on aircraft. Angie worked part time to help out financially as they never had lots of money. Giles rose through the ranks of the airline and although he never earned masses of money, it was enough and they were happy. However Giles got promoted and for several years had not gone anywhere near an aircraft and he no longer enjoyed his job. He hated the shift work, the drive to Heathrow and wanted to get back to working with his hands, preferably on aircraft but definitely not in the thankless and stressful management role in which he now found himself. The good salary helped but deep down, he was just plain unhappy.

Then in 2012 I sat him and Angie down and did some number crunching and we worked out that if Giles could earn £20,000 per year instead of the £45k he was then earning for the airline he could leave. Angie wasn't sure at first because they had just started to not have to worry about money but, using the principles in this book, the truth was inescapable. Giles could leave his job and by earning £20,000 per year their standard of living would not change.

With a sharp intake of breath and a little persuading Angie they took the plunge. Giles semi-retired 5 years early, age 60.

A few months later I visited them. Giles had the biggest grin on his face and told me that within two weeks he had seen a job advertised locally working for a retired airline pilot who now ran a combined commercial property and farm, so he needed someone to maintain the whole show - including buiding a new micro light aircraft. The salary was £21,500.

A few weeks after that I bumped in to Giles at Reading service station. Giles and Angie had booked three holidays together and Giles had also bought the digital SLR camera he really wanted and was spending time photographing the classic aircraft and vintage cars that he so enjoyed. He's happy and thoroughly enjoying life.

That makes me happy. That's cool. That's why I do what I do.

UPDATE: *I met Giles and Angie a few months ago. Angie has seen Giles enjoying himself so much that she wants to retire too. Giles isn't too sure – he's worried she might give him a long list of jobs to do around the house! These days, they laugh a lot, spend time with their new grandchild, and are just plain happy. They do not have loads of money but they have something far more important. True wealth: happiness. Lots and lots of happiness and all the stress has gone.*

Stories like this is why I get out of bed in the morning, why I do what I do for a living. That's why I had to write this book; if only one person changes their life as result of this, I'm done for this lifetime, and I'll die happy.

"The chief value of money lies in the fact that one lives in a world in which it is overestimated."

H L MENCKEN

Chapter Four: **The Four Pillars of Investing**

The four pillars for understanding investing in order to get the most from it are as follows:

1. Risk and reward are inextricably linked

2. You are not capable of beating the market

3. No one can time the market

4. Owning a small number of stocks is dangerous.

There is a little more to it than that, but if we look primarily at stock markets there are some facts you need to know.

Markets are generally efficient, i.e. everything that can be known about all stocks is generally known, especially in this age of technology. Stock brokers and fund managers will tell you all about the research that they do in to the fundamentals of the company in whose stock they will invest your money, but the reality is that there are any number of fund managers/ brokers that will do exactly the same thing. There is very little real evidence that fund managers and stock brokers add any real value over an extended period of time.

Also, if what they are recommending is such a great investment, why on earth are they telling you about it??

Remember that all markets are a zero sum game; for every buyer there will be a seller and vice versa. Stock brokers and fund managers will all contend that because of their systems, processes, and/or superior knowledge, they will outperform the market. However they can't all be right, it doesn't make sense. The facts (we LOVE facts) do not bear out their claims.

At this point I have probably started a riot somewhere - but I don't care, because the facts speak for themselves. If you want to try to pick the next "hot stock" then please, go ahead. If you would rather sift through fund managers and give your money to them to manage for you, please go ahead. If you want to pay someone to do it for you then please do so.

But never forget that they charge you for doing this stuff. That it's your money they spend which means that they have to be able to make even MORE money to justify their fees.

Charges Are Your Enemy

When you invest in anything, including shares, we know that risk and reward are inextricably linked. Therefore you expect an additional return for taking investment risk. This is called the "equity risk premium". Depending on which publication you read a very reasonable estimate of the equity risk premium is around 4% over investing in cash. In other words, if you can readily achieve a return of say 2% by investing in cash then you should expect a return of 6% (2% + 4%) by investing in shares.

That's it, and so when you read stories about the long term benefits of investing in the stock market do NOT think that you will achieve double digit returns over time. You won't - that is not the way the system is built. That may happen in the short term but it won't happen in the long term.

So now let's look at charges. We need to look at **visible** and **invisible** charges.

Visible Charges

These are usually the fund managers' charges which can be typically around 1% to 2% with 1.5% being a common charge. There are other visible charges that are relatively minor, such as dilution levy, which is not a major factor. The most common name for these visible charges is the **TER** or **Total Expense Ratio**. However when we drill down beyond the TER there is another underworld of charges that remain invisible and shrouded in mystery. These are the charges the fund managers don't want you to know about. They are insidious and eat away silently at your returns.

These invisible costs can be summarized as **Portfolio Turnover Charges**. These are:

Stamp Duty: Every time your fund manager buys a fresh share in your portfolio they have to pay 0.5% Stamp Duty (on UK shares).

Spread: When you buy and sell foreign currency you lose money (which is how the vendor makes money). It's called "spread". The same applies to shares. You pay your fund manager to trade shares on your behalf, which is how they aim to make money for you. So, they may sell, for example, British Telecom shares in the expectation that they can buy them back later on more cheaply. The trouble is that this buy and sell exercise is subject to the dreaded spread. This is not a major issue for major shares such as BT, BP, Glaxo Smith Kline and so on with spreads around 0.1% but for smaller stocks spreads can reach 2%, 3%, 4%. For shares or funds in more volatile markets such as Emerging Markets, spreads can reach double figures.

Trading Costs: This one's straightforward and is simply the fees charged by stock brokers for buying and selling stock.

If a fund buys and sells every single share in its portfolio in a year then the fund is defined as having a portfolio turnover rate of 100%. A typical portfolio turnover rate is between 50% and 200%.

A portfolio turnover rate of 100% is estimated (by the UK Regulator the FCA) to cost 1.8% a year. The FCA is currently considering its position about illegal use of broker commissions payable to fund managers over the last year. Oh and by the way the amount involved is £1.5 billion. That's £1,500,000,000.

That's known as "a lot".

Well, hang on a minute. If the TER is 1.5%, and the cost of Portfolio Turnover is, as an example, 1.8% then the charges are up to an eye watering 3.3% before a financial planner is paid (the good guys – they give it to you straight). This therefore means that you, the poor, hapless investor, is the one taking all the risk.

Don't take my word for it: Warren Buffet is one of the world's wealthiest individuals and founded Berkshire Hathaway fund, one of the industry's biggest stock holdings. Here's an extract from Warren's recent letter to his trustees as to how to invest his fortune when he dies:

> *My advice to the trustee couldn't be more simple: Put 10% of the cash in short-term government bonds and 90% in a very low-cost S&P 500 index fund. (I suggest Vanguard's.) I believe the trust's long-term results from this policy will be superior to those attained by most investors — whether pension funds, institutions or individuals — who employ high-fee managers.*
>
> *Both individuals and institutions will constantly be urged to be active by those who profit from giving advice or effecting transactions. The resulting frictional costs can be huge and, for investors in aggregate, devoid of benefit. So ignore the chatter, keep your costs minimal, and invest in stocks as you would in a farm.*

We agree.

So why are these charges important and why do you NEED to

know about them? The answer is straightforward and lies in the power of compounding and time. Let's look at an example:

Three investors each put £10,000 into three different funds. The funds are identical in every respect except charges: Fund A charges 0.25% per year; Fund B charges 0.75% per year; and Fund C charges 1.50 % per year. Assume each fund returns 6% per year. After 30 years, the value of Fund C will have grown to more than £36,000. Fund B will have grown to more than £45,000. And Fund A? It will have grown to more than £53,000. That's a difference of over 47%.

Why such a big difference? The total expenses of the investments, that's the only variable.

You can see the real advantage of keeping investment costs low, and how that advantage becomes more pronounced over time. That's it. Charges are your enemy. Avoid.

At this point a fund manager or proponent of active fund manager will say the magic words "yes, but…" and present you with any number of statistical models and evidence that they will make you more money than the market. We call that stuff "financial porn". When you see the adverts on those huge posters at railway stations or airports ask yourself this question: "I wonder who is paying for that advertisement in such a prominent and presumably expensive location?"

My response to the active argument is simple. If I invest with an active fund manager I am taking more risk (back to the risk, reward formula) and so I expect a greater return for the extra layer of risk. Therefore Mr Fund Manager I want you to sign the following statement before I invest with you:

Dear Sir (they're always polite)

I guarantee to make you more money than the market, plus my fees, plus the extra return you are entitled to for investing with me, year in year out, till death us do part.

Somehow I don't think they will sign the declaration.

Stick to basic principles. YOU are entitled to the return for the risk you are taking. No-one else. It's your money; make sure you hang on to it.

"Compound interest is the eighth wonder of the world. He who understands it, earns it... he who doesn't... pays it.

ALBERT EINSTEIN

Chapter Five: **Compound Interest & Volatility**

Why should I invest in the stock market anyway? Quite simply, to make money out of the capitalist system.

It really is that simple. You invest with companies that seek to manufacture stuff or provide services, who, in order to make it attractive for you to invest, seek to increase the value of your investment and also pay you a share of profits. That's pretty much it at the simplest level.

By investing in the stock market you can invest in well run household names such as BP, Glaxo, BT and so on. You can also invest in poorly run companies, which may or may not turnaround (sometimes called Special Situations). It's easier than starting your own BP/Glaxo/BT and means that you can sit on the beach while other people make money for you.

This is where the traditional reasons for investing in the stock market stand up to scrutiny. There are any number of graphs and studies that demonstrate the long term benefits of investing in the stock market - perhaps one of the best known is the Barclays Equity Gilt study of long term performance:

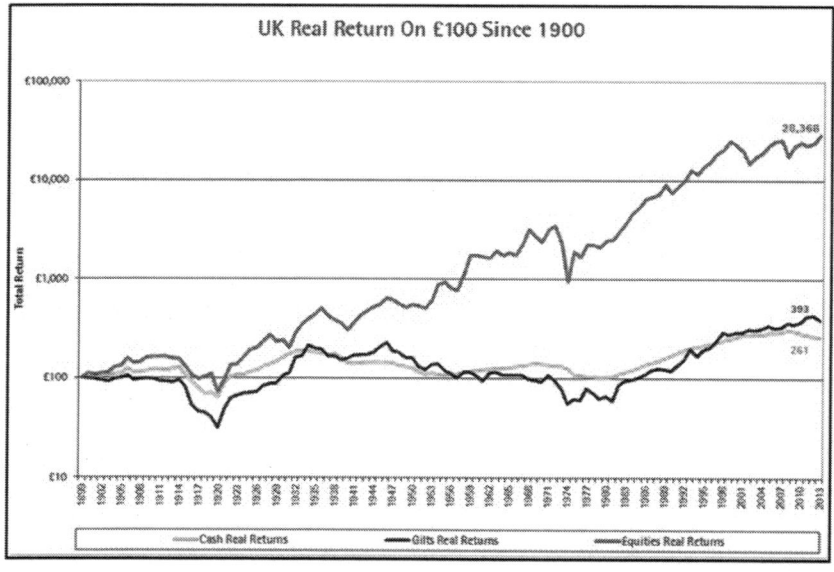

This chart shows the real returns that would have been achieved on a £100 investment made at the start of 1900, assuming that the returns were re-invested annually.

A £100 investment in UK equities would be worth £28,368 in real terms (after allowing for the effects of inflation); £100 invested in Gilts would be worth just £393 and cash even less at £261.

In other words, the real returns on equities have been on average 5.1% a year compared to 1.2% for Gilts.

The Hidden Money Maker: Reinvested Dividends

Reinvesting dividends is one of the most underrated hidden heroes of making money from investing in shares. One of the principle reasons for investing in shares has been to share in the profits of the companies in which your fund is invested. Dividends are the payment of a share of the profits a company makes. It is separate from the increase or decrease in the capital value of those same shares. (The market determines the value of those shares.)

Rather than simply taking your dividends as cash, you can use it the money buy more shares, giving the potential to earn even more dividends in the future. As this process is repeated, a small initial sum can eventually become much larger.

For example, if £10,000 was invested in the FTSE-All share Index in July 1994, it would be worth £24,705 today without dividend reinvestment. However, if all of the dividends were reinvested, that investment would now be worth £48,230. That's over 95% more.

That's it. Reinvested dividends can significantly boots the value of your investments in the long term.

Is There a Catch?

Yes, there's a catch. It's called **volatility**.

It's all very well trotting out figures that show what has happened in the past but as we all know, past performance is no guide to the future.

However, past human behaviour **is** a guide to the future of human behaviour: human nature does not change fundamentally and, unless capitalism fails completely (or there is a nuclear war), then in the long term the basic principles will apply.

If there were to be a nuclear war we'll all be fried anyway - though you'd probably be happier watching that mushroom cloud having made sure you'd done all the stuff in your life that you wanted to!

When making your own plans for your future you must take in to account volatility; be prepared to accept lower returns in return for greater certainty.

The chart below shows the value of the FTSE100 Index from December 1983 to August 2010:

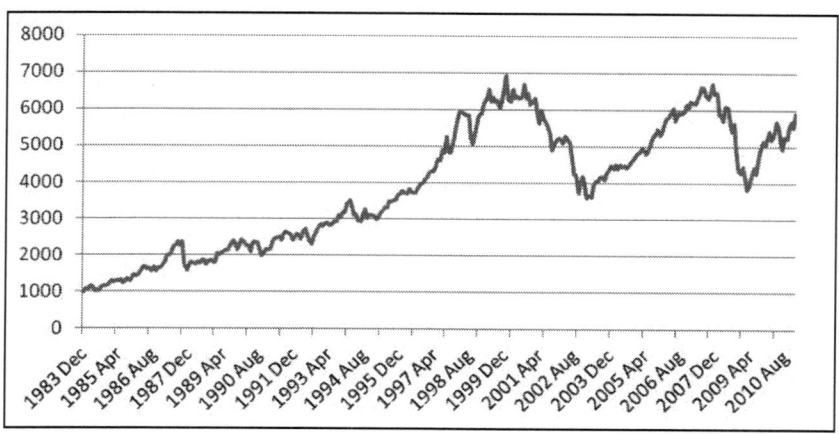

You'd probably be pleased with the returns had you invested in the 1980s or early 1990s as well as 2003 or 2009; but what if you had invested in 1999 or 2000? Your investment would have pretty quickly fallen in value and by 2010 would still not have recovered.

My point here is that there are so many charts that will always show the benefits of long term investment in the stock market - the Barclays Equity Guilt Study on the previous page shows clearly why you should invest in the stock market for the long term. Even the switched-on financial planners out there who use financial modelling software (including the author of course) will come up with a rate of investment return that is needed in order to make the plan work. However the one variable that you MUST take in to account is volatility. It's all very well relying on the returns from stock markets over the long term when the returns are relatively predictable, but short term movements in the value of investments can do serious financial and emotional damage.

You MUST carefully consider the effect of short term fluctuations in the value of investments. This risk can be mitigated in several ways, for example including a mixture of asset classes within a portfolio to "turn the heat down". Also it is always wise to make sure that short term needs for capital expenditure are taken care of as well as income requirements for the first few years of your plan. This can be taken care of with shorter term investments. There are other ways of mitigating the risks of volatility but they are beyond the scope of this book.

The big point here is that it is all very well saying that stock markets will go up by around 5% to 7% a year, but what if your investments go down by 20% in one year? It's very well saying that the investment horizon is 5 years upwards, but at that point what you really care about is "s**t, my money is worth 20% less than this time last year. What if I run out of money...?"

In my view, the effect of volatility is too frequently glossed over and you must get very honest with yourself about this; how would you REALLY feel if your investments went down by 20%? It's only a few years since the last time that actually happened. How did you feel during the crash of 2008/2009? Really, how did you feel? If you were scared and worried you need to look at the volatility of your portfolio, accept the prospect of lower returns in return for greater peace of mind.

Time is a great investor and so you must always keep back enough cash and/or income to be able to ride out the inevitable storms.

You MUST be able to watch the news, see that the markets have collapsed, think "hey ho", get up make a cup of tea and get on with finishing the crossword puzzle (or Sudoku of course).

Compound Interest: The Eighth Wonder of the World

Compound interest needs to be "mixed" with time in order to be effective. Time and compound interest are two of the most powerful forces working in your favour when you invest in stocks and shares.

Initial Investment: **£10,000**

Years	Rate of Growth				
	5%	**6%**	**10%**	**11%**	**15%**
5	£12,763	£13,382	£16,105	£16,851	£20,114
10	£16,289	£17,908	£25,937	£28,394	£40,456
15	£20,789	£23,966	£41,772	£47,846	£81,371
20	£26,533	£32,071	£67,275	£80,623	£163,665
25	£33,864	£42,919	£108,347	£135,855	£329,190
30	£43,219	£57,435	£174,494	£228,923	£662,118

We could drone on and on about the magic of compound interest, but there's no point. You'd get bored - though as I said at the beginning, boring is good. Make money predictably is what it is all about, and compound interest is one great way of doing just that.

Hint:

Ponder this. If the power of compound interest is so fundamental to investing over the longer term, then it follows that even minor differences in returns are important. Therefore is charges are significant then they simply rob you of some of the benefits of compound interest. Yet more grist to the "avoid charges at all costs" mantra.

"OK, first rule of Wall Street.

Nobody - and I don't care
if you're Warren Buffet or
Jimmy Buffet - nobody knows
if a stock's going up, down or
*#$&ing sideways, least of all
stock brokers."

MARK HANNA – THE WOLF OF WALL STREET

Chapter Six: **The Myth of Pound Cost Averaging**

This is an old chestnut that often appears in those money makeovers you see in the newspapers or the financial advice columns in the press, often by so-called experts. Sacrilege I hear you cry! Pound cost averaging; the saviour of the regular saver. Nope. Sorry.

Pound cost averaging works, but in a narrow range of circumstances but is, in general, irrelevant - and here's why.

For those who have not heard of this phenomenon it goes something like this. If you invest in shares in Widgets PLC and you are not sure if the price of the shares is going to go down (or up for that matter) then why not buy a few shares each month? The supposed magic then happens like this:

Suppose I decide to invest £100 a month in shares in Widgets PLC and in month one the shares are £1 each. It therefore follows that I get 100 shares. Right so far. Hang in there.

Then in month two I invest another £100 but, horror of horrors, the shares have halved in value (and price) to 50p, and I shout "sacre bleu" as I realize that my month one shares are now worth a paltry £50. However I console myself in the knowledge that in month two I buy 200 shares for my £100.

In month three, double sacre bleu. The market in Widgets PLC shares collapses further to 25p a share and my month one shares are now worth a big, fat 25 quid. EEK! However, undeterred, I trudge onwards to my financial doom and carry on investing but console myself with picking up 400 shares in month three at 25p a pop for my 100 quid.

Then the light bulb gets replaced at the end of the pound-cost-averaging-tunnel and the shares recover to £1 each. So I am somewhat happier that my £100 has now bought 100 shares.

Then in month 5 someone turns the light bulb back on and the shares increase in price to £1.25.

Phew! I now have 880 shares for which I paid £500 but now those very same shares are worth £1.25 each so my investment is now worth £1,100. Incroyable! (I have no idea why I did that in French). I've made £600 due to the miracle of Pound Cost Averaging. (In case you hadn't guessed it, this example is exaggerated to make the point.)

It works! We're saved!

Well, yes and er, no.

And here's why. (Sorry to pierce the bubble.)

The first bubble-piercing fact is that yep, it works but it also works exactly the same but in the OPPOSITE DIRECTION in a RISING market!! To make PCA work you need a falling market for a fair amount of time (1/2/3 years) followed by a rising market. Yet again, that's trying to call the market – and do NOT try to second guess the market. That's called "a waste of time and energy".

But that's not all. Here's more bad news for the Pound Cost Averaging disciples...

Let's use an example.

Suppose you put £1000 a month in to your shares/unit trust/ISA/whatever and the price fluctuates. The price goes down. You call your financial planner and shout "yikes". Never fear says he, it's fine because of pound cost averaging.

Now let's add in another piece of information. You are investing £1,000 a month and **YOU ALREADY HAVE £200,000 IN THE FUND.** If the price of the units/shares you are buying has just gone down by 20% do you REALLY CARE that your £1000 per month is buying shares at a 20% discount. No you bloody well don't, I would suggest. What you REALLY care about is the fact that your £200,000 has just gone down in value by £40,000! Who cares that you saved £200 (compared to last month) on your monthly investment of £1,000 – you've lost £40,000! Ouch.

So here's the rub. Pound cost averaging has an effect, but ONLY in the early stages of a regular savings plan in to an asset where the price fluctuates. Eventually the fluctuation in the price of the share/units is of hardly any relevance. And it ONLY works if the price falls initially and then rises. If it goes the other way it works against you.

Sorry folks, it's all down to mathematics.

Therefore the simplest solution is always the best. DON'T try to outsmart the markets. Define your plan, your attitude to risk and your asset allocation (which eggs in which baskets), buy low cost funds that capture the market to do the required job and then park it. Go for lunch, play golf, go on holiday, spend time with your (grand)children, work through your bucket list. These are all a better use of your time.

What's important is time IN the market, not TIMING the market. For example, if we look at the past 10 years for the MSCI World Index from December 2002 to December 2012 - if you had stayed invested the whole time your return would have been 68.96%. If you had missed the best 30 days your return would have been -49.08%. If you had missed the best 20 days your return would have been -32.19%, and -4.64% for the crime of missing only the 10 best days.

So missing the best 10 days would have cost you a return of 73.60%.

Source: Fidelity

The solution:

Stick to simple stuff. DON'T try and second-guess the market. By all means invest on a regular basis but what you need is a sound fund with the correct risk characteristics for your emotional state, your plans and your requirements. If you try to second-guess the market, you will usually be right about half of the time. The trick is to get in to the market with a correctly constructed investment portfolio and enjoy your spare time instead of trying to outsmart the market. We call this "stupidity prevention".

If you use this stuff in your planning you will win the investment game. You'll irritate a lot of people along the way, such as fund managers, bank managers, but who cares? Its YOUR money. Invest it wisely and then spend it. Enjoy it. That's what it's for.

A lot of people will urge you to put some money in a bank and in fact – within reason – this is very good advice. But don't go overboard. Remember: what you are doing is giving your money to somebody else to hold on to and I think that it is worth keeping in mind that the businessmen who run banks are so worried out holding on to things that they put little chains on all their pens.

CASE STUDY THREE: Tony

This time I consider that I failed.

A potential new client, Tony, found us through the internet and came in for the initial "getting to know you" meeting. We went through the usual financial stuff and then I talked about lifestyle financial planning, which is what I do. It's what I enjoy doing and what I get a kick out of delivering. It's why I get up in the morning; I love making a difference to people's lives. Real life changing stuff and not the dry boring money stuff.

Tony works in IT and is very successful. He earns over £150,000 a year, had paid off their mortgage (he is married with a couple of young children) and wanted a review of his various pensions. He had prepared several spreadsheets of performance figures and wondered why some of his funds had done better than others. I looked at what he had done and it was some basic stuff where he was not comparing like with like... He just wanted that bit fixing and wasn't at all interested in a full, proper financial plan. I said he could do it himself if he liked and gave him the details of a couple of online brokers who could offer him what he wanted. I also gave him some pointers on what sort of funds to look at. Yawn.

We carried on chatting and got on the subject of his dreams; in particular, his dream of becoming a commercial helicopter pilot. Learning to fly helicopters had also been on my bucket list for a long time, and so I learnt to fly 5 years ago. It was one of the best things I have ever done. I flew over swamps in Florida at 30 feet, landed on top of a skyscraper in Fort Lauderdale, flew in British Columbia, landing on top of a mountain surrounded by snow, flew over Sydney Opera House, the Harbour Bridge and Manly Beach. It was all fabulous and I remember it like it was yesterday.

Tony started telling me how he really wanted to become a commercial helicopter pilot and had started the CPPL course. I asked him more about what he wanted to do with his life. It turned out that he could take a couple of years off work as they had enough cash in the bank, Tony could go through the pilot training and if it didn't work out he could easily go back to his old career. It would not make any really difference to their long term plans. It's a cliché, but in my view it is better to have loved and lost than to never have loved at all.

However Tony kept coming back to the blasted funds he had in his pension plans, waffling on about fund selection and asset allocation. I even tried to tempt him with the knowledge that I had a commercial helicopter training captain as a client who specialises in training the new batch of desperately needed helicopter pilots for North Sea companies. I could have got him a job living his dream. It would take him a year to find out if he could cut the mustard and make it. His wife was up for it and would have supported him in his quest.

Again and again he returned to the funds in his pensions and eventually the meeting drew to close. I asked him to think about what we do but I never heard from him again. I hope for his sake that he eventually does live his dream, stops sweating the small stuff and never looks back with regret.

As for me, although I wonder whether I could have done better in the meeting, I have to let it go and hope he sees the light one day.

"There are people who have money and people who are rich.

COCO CHANEL

Chapter Seven: **Other People's Money, Gearing & Multiple Streams of Income**

Lets start with gearing.

At its simplest this is simply borrowing money to invest. By doing so you hope (and presumably expect) the value of the asset to increase in value so that after all the costs you make more money than if you do not make use of gearing. The simplest example is buying your own home, assuming that you have done so or are planning to do so in the future.

Suppose you have £100,000 you want to invest or use to buy your home. You take out a mortgage for example for £400,000 and then toddle off and buy a house to live in for £500,000.

If the property goes up by say 10% in a year then the property goes up in value by £50,000 but you have only invested £100,000 so you have achieved a return of 50% on your original investment.

Genius. Love it.

Wait it gets even better. Suppose you then get someone else to pay for the mortgage costs, the investment has cost you nothing. Right?

Well, yes, though there are a few points to note:

It only works in a rising market; witness the events of 2008 (which so many seem to have forgotten about already). If we take the same example then if the property value falls by the same 10% you have LOST 50% or £50,000.

Hmmm, not so attractive.

Also, if you have borrowed to make the investment then you have to factor in the cost of the interest that will be charged on the loan.

Bearing in mind that the interest rates on buy to let mortgages are around 3% to 5% and the income return on a pretty standard buy to let property is 4.5% ish (yes, yes I know there are variations – for example student lets), then your return becomes almost entirely dependent on the increase in the value of the property.

If you are buying a property to rent out then you also need to take account of the following:

- Landlords insurance
- Safety costs – PAT testing, gas supply testing and certification, ditto electricity
- Accountancy costs
- Income tax on the rental income – (although this is offset by mortgage interest and other expenses)
- Capital Gains Tax when (if) you come to sell
- Liquidity – how quickly can the property be sold if you need the cash? (Easy at the moment I know but twas not always thus.)
- Voids – periods when the property is empty
- Repairs and replacements – washing machines, fridges etc.
- The place getting damaged – regular redecoration and maintenance
- Default – i.e. the tenants don't cough up the rent
- Stress...

Beware interest only loans to finance buy to let property. The minute you opt for an interest only loan (the US calls them "liar loans") you have made absolutely sure that your only return can come from the increase in the value of the property.

We recommend making sure that the mortgage gets paid off over time, either on a pay as you go basis (repayment mortgage) or the "full stop" method where you use some kind of savings vehicle to pay off the loan at, for example, your retirement date.

The point of all of this is to make use of OPM or **other people's money**; i.e. to get other people to give you their money in return for the use of an asset that you have purchased.

To Sell or Not to Sell?

I am often quizzed about Capital Gains Tax on the sale of a property. Yes, I know how this works and how to do the calculations, but my response is always initially the same. I ask; why would you sell? If the property generates an income stream, and let's face it, it's income you need when you retire, why sell?

Of course, there can be times when it makes sense to sell, depending on your personal circumstances. I often find that the older people get the more they seek simplicity and freedom from aggravation and so they will often dispose of investment property at that time - and we help them to invest the proceeds.

In addition, there is probably one more thing you need to bear in mind:

Let's assume that the property is let, paid for and generating a rental yield of say 5%. Let's assume you are a basic rate tax payer paying 20% tax on the rent, making the net return in terms of income 4%. Then you need to deduct the expenses associated with letting - say that comes to another 0.5% then your net return after tax is 3.5%. All well and good.

However it is not that difficult to create hassle free investment portfolios that, over the longer term, generate AFTER TAX returns of 4% to 5% with relatively low exposure to investment risk.

Why is this so? Simply put, it's because part of your total return is tied up in the bricks and mortar investment – you *are* actually receiving a higher return than the net figure of 3.5% mentioned earlier, but part of it is reflected in the increase in value of the property. Unfortunately eating bricks and mortar is challenging and so there comes a time when using property to generate income makes less sense. However, as usual, it always comes down to YOU; the most important piece of the jigsaw.

It's what's important to YOU that matters.

I like property as an investment; I invest in property as well as the stock market. I still own one of my old houses which I rent out, along with some commercial property. (Returns on commercial property can be much higher – but that's outside the scope of this book.) I know how it works. It can be an excellent addition to any investment portfolio.

As an aside gearing can be used to fund share investments, through the use of options but, again, that is outside the scope of this book. Please remember that the possibility of greater returns ALWAYS comes with the price tag of additional risk. There are no grey areas here. Greater returns mean greater risk. THAT'S THE RULE. End of.

If you really, really must have a dabble...

For those of you who really, really want to have a go at investing in the stock market and are seeking to potentially make higher returns there are any number of gambling dens masquerading as investment nirvana, often CFDs or Contracts For Difference (we call them Contracts For Disaster).

They aren't our bag. We keep it simple, follow a few simple rules and both we and our clients make money.

However if you really want to have a bash we recommend setting aside a sum of money that you can absolutely afford to lose. For example, £5,000 if you have a portfolio of £500,000 in pensions, cash and so on - i.e. 1% of your capital.

Then go and check out a method of trading called "**trading the channel**" or "**channel trading**". Get familiar with one of the best online software packages around and enjoy. Its complex but you may enjoy it. Our standard line is that it should come with a free anorak because you need to get very knowledgeable and learn to drive some fairly complex software and learn a new language to boot.

It makes sense to trade the largest (by some margin) stock market in the world, namely the US. With that in mind, check out www.worden.com. Their Telechart software is excellent and there are loads of instructional videos you can watch. You'll need to set up a U$ denominated trading account to run alongside the software. If you fancy it by all means give it a go.

Apart from that you are on your own. Not our bag I'm afraid. Life's too short.

Chapter Eight: **Be Prepared to Burn Your Money**

Don't worry. This is not about popping wads of cash in to the Aga or using the folding stuff to kick start your wood burning stove. This IS about not getting hung up on retaining your capital when you retire. Of course, you may want to make sure all of your capital is intact when you die, but in my experience, most clients agree that their children will want them to enjoy their money, the fruits of mum and dad's hard-earned labours. If there is any left over that would be a bonus. (Of course I do occasionally come up against money grabbing offspring – makes me want to throw up.)

The best way to explain this is to use an example. Suppose you need to generate an income of £50,000 in retirement. Can we please ignore tax, just for now? Humour me.

If you achieve a return of 5% then you need a capital sum of £1m in order to generate your income of £50,000. So far so good.

However, suppose you are 60 years old and you require the same income of £50,000, and you achieve a return of 5%. If however you are happy for the pot to be empty by the time you die at let's say age 90, then you only need a starting capital sum of £768,622.

That's £231,378 less and much more manageable. Let's also suppose that your house is worth £1M at age 60, then if house price inflation is a modest 4% then by the same age, i.e. age 90 your house will be worth £3.24M. In my experience that is more than enough to provide a meaningful inheritance for your children.

So the trick is to accept that you will use up your capital, preferably at a pre-determined rate and then leave your other assets as your inheritance for your children.

I find that conceptually this works really well. In practice, I find that the biggest issue has nothing to do with money. The biggest problem is emotional. We all tend to spend our lives saving for our retirement, but to reach the magic age and then to start *spending* the capital and watching your bank balances go DOWN (down for goodness sake!!) then that can do serious emotional damage and can take some getting used to.

However, provided that you have planned properly, not told yourself porkies and stick to the rules you should be able to die happy in the knowledge that the last cheque you ever wrote bounced...

So be prepared for the emotions associated with spending capital; it can take a while to get used to. I have handled a lot of retirements and I reckon it takes around two years to get used to the idea - I have no scientific evidence for this, just loads of real life experience.

CASE STUDY FOUR: James & Suzanne

James is a marketing specialist. He is well respected in his field that is around paper based advertising in magazines. He was always very good at it and enjoys his work.

His wife Suzanne was a teacher but she had retired around 10 years ago. They enjoyed a great standard of living but had always invested well; taking advantage of all of the standard tax breaks on pensions, ISAs and so on.

However now that James was (a very healthy and active) 65 year old, Suzanne wanted him to stop working and spend more time with her and their grandchildren. Suzanne wanted them to give even more money to their children even after the gifts they had already made. James was not so sure. He was still nervous about giving away even more money. What if they ran out of the stuff? They love travelling and wanted to do more of it. They also love going to the theatre and especially enjoy going to the opera.

James still enjoyed his work but was working long hours, 4 to 5 days a week and still travelling occasionally in connection with his work.

Once again I crunched the numbers and 5 years ago sat them in my office and went through all the mathematics and was able to prove that it didn't really matter how well their investments performed. They could stick the whole lot under the mattress and James would still be able to retire and yet enjoy exactly the same standard of living as if he continued to work.

Even if they gave more money to their children it still worked.

Then, around half way through the meeting after I had proved they would never run out of money, Suzanne looked and James and pointed a finger at him, and with a great big smile on her face, said "see, I told you that you could retire…"

At that point James literally turned pale and said "yes, but I remember when I was a child, my mum and dad had to break open my money box so that they could buy a loaf of bread and a bottle of milk so that we could eat that night…."

And that was the block. That was the real reason that James couldn't quite let go of the need to work. Sometimes it's not about the money. Sometimes there is something else stopping us having the life we want and deserve. Sometimes it's the emotional stuff but that's a whole subject in itself. Maybe one day I'll write another book about it…

In the end James dropped to working 4 days a week, then 3, then 2 and now does the odd bit of consultancy now and then, but only if a project interests him and is fun. I think Suzanne quite likes that arrangement because if they were together 24 hours a day it would drive them both nuts.

They gave some more money to their children, and they have just come back from a fabulous trip around Vietnam and Cambodia. Suzanne loves driving her brand new mini and James is enjoying his new BMW 5 series.

They still go the theatre and the opera. They eat at very, very nice restaurants and fly business class. Love it!

"My friends, money is not all. It is not money that will mend a broken heart or reassemble the fragments of a dream. Money cannot brighten the hearth nor repair the portals of a shattered home. I refer, of course, to Confederate Money."

ARTEMUS WARD

Chapter Nine: **Why the Government Hates Trusts**

This is a really odd one to get your head around.

Trusts are a sort of financial treasure chest with certain rules around them in terms of law and tax. The "problem" is that they can keep the tax man at bay for long periods of time, indeed anything up to 125 years (unless it's a charity).

Trusts came in to being during the Crusades - when the Crusaders toddled off to do their thing, they left someone in charge of their assets/gaff/land etc. while they were away. They "trusted" someone to look after their stuff. And that's pretty much it.

Now, let's look at the concept of "the Government always gets all of your money", and then look at ways to stop it or at least to stop it for a considerable amount of time.

Suppose you buy a new car. You pay VAT on the purchase price which goes to the Government. The balance goes partially to the dealership where you bought the car. They pay Corporation Tax (to the Government) on any profits they make and pay the rest to the manufacturer. The dealership pays salaries, utilities, suppliers and so on. The manufacturer buys stuff to build the cars. It also pays salaries that, er, get taxed.

So all this money arrives at the Government in the form of Income Tax, National Insurance, Corporation Tax, Capital Gains Tax, VAT, Stamp Duty... (are you getting the idea yet?)

The Government is the biggest employer in the country. They pay out benefits, the cost of the NHS, all those Civil Servants, doctors, nurses, dentists, police, fire-fighters and so on. They also pay for infrastructure such as hospitals and roads. But, hang on; they also employ people who use their wages to buy goods and services - so if you think it through, all the Government actually does is to **redistribute the money**. Eventually it all comes back to the Government. Nice work if you can get it. Oh and it's all enforceable in law.

"Aha" I hear you cry. **I will save it and they will not get their hands on it.** Well, the only way that works is if you never spend it and don't die. Assuming that you aren't immortal then your heirs will pay Inheritance Tax when you die and the whole system still gets its hands on your money.

Now, I don't really have a problem this because the reason for a strong government is to prevent anarchy and to stop us all having to be violent just to buy stuff from the supermarket. However, trusts, those personalised money treasure chests are a great way to minimise the amount of your money that gets paid to the Government. It only works for 125 years though. Even then the Government tax any income received by most trusts at up to 45%. There are also additional charges every 10 years, but this area is complex and requires professional advice.

There are two main ways to make sure that you use trusts to keep money away from the Government. The first is to get the trust to invest in assets that do not generate any income in a taxable form. These are imaginatively called "non income producing assets".

The second is to NOT take money out of the trust directly but to **borrow** money from the trust. This has all sorts of advantages concerning Inheritance Tax planning; protecting your money from future sons/daughters-in-law pushing off with your money if your kids get divorced; and finally Care Home fees planning.

Trusts are relatively complex and you should get specialist advice but the main point to take away here is they are useful for keeping the Government's hands off your own or your family's money for as long as possible. They are also useful for controlling your assets and who gets your money.

"What if nothing exists and money is an illusion? Then I definitely overpaid for my carpet."

WOODY ALLEN

Chapter Ten: **Marketing and How it Costs You Money - Seeing Through the Illusion**

Very few financial planning books give an insight into the system but it's around you all the time. It's not sinister as depicted in the movie "*The Matrix*" but never the less it does exist. Here are some examples:

In the supermarket – buy one get one half price. Really?!! It's a lie or at least a half truth designed to get you to spend more in that moment. Become aware. Change your thinking. The label should say "its £££ if you buy one and ££££ if you buy two". Have you noticed how more supermarkets now have whole rows of produce devoted to BOGOF or similar? It's all about getting you to spend more money. You can buy in to it if you like but just become aware. Ask yourself "do I really need two of those? Will I just throw them away? Am I being manipulated in to buying more than I need? Can I buy loose tomatoes/ potatoes/unwashed potatoes (that taste better anyway) for a lower price? Will I actually eat them?"

When making a larger purchase, for example furniture - IGNORE ANY LABELS THAT SAY 50%/70%/20% off/last few days/2 chairs free. Simply ask yourself "at this price, does this represent good value for money to me and do I really want to buy this item/these items? Are they what I was looking for?" If the answer is yes, buy and go home happy. If you are not sure, leave it 24 hours, go home and then if you still want the sofa/ chairs/table then go back and buy them. If not then you can have fun looking around elsewhere.

Don't forget that many furniture stores make more money out of selling credit than selling furniture. If they offer interest free credit then ask for a discount if you just pay cash. You'd be amazed how often the answer will be yes.

Beware the power of marketing. Billions and billions of pounds are spent on marketing to get you to buy stuff that makes you feel more attractive/wealthy/confident etc. If you buy this perfume (endorsed by a celebrity) you will be fitter, healthier, more attractive… That's called "bulls**t". If you like the smell, great, go for it. If you are not sure leave it and let the moment pass.

Beware designer clothes – This includes designer clothes outlets, designer bags, designer shoes, limited edition anything. A designer handbag is still a handbag. It will NOT make you prettier, more attractive and more interesting. It WILL make you poorer. If it will make you happier and the price is worth paying, then great. Go ahead. If you are not sure, then apply the

24 hour rule. Here's a cool trick I learnt a few years ago: empty out a tin of baked beans or similar. Put your credit card in tin and fill the tin with water and pop it in the freezer till frozen. When you spot something to buy that you are not sure about take the tin out of the freezer and wait for it to defrost. This will take around 12 hours or so; if at that point you still want to buy the item, then go ahead. If not, then look at the money you have saved.

This is NOT about being tight, or a complete spendthrift. It's about making choices that are right for you and taking your power of choice away from the marketers whose primary aim is to make money for them, their company and their shareholders.

Beware of easy credit.

It's everywhere, all designed to relieve you of your hard earned cash. It never seems so expensive when the price is so much "a month". Debt keeps you working, keeps you in the system so you have to work to repay the debt. Avoid debt unless it can make you money (see gearing in chapter seven).

Short term debt such as credit cards can best be described (in gullible hands) as **"consumer cocaine"**.

Understand "**post purchase dissonance**" or "**buyer's remorse**". Why do you think eBay is so successful and so full of items that are new/nearly new? Of course, this makes eBay a great place to buy your stuff – have a look, if you don't use it already. You can also sell stuff you don't need (or give to charity). If you haven't read it, worn it, watched it or interacted with it in the last 12-18 months - get rid of it. You will look back in the not too distant future and wonder why you had such a tough time letting go.

Better still don't buy the stuff in the fist place. Do you really *really* need that fancy SLR camera, when a standard digital compact will do everything you want to... Do you really need three versions of what is virtually the same coat... If you want it - great go ahead and buy it, but just double check that you really want this damn thing in the first place and keep your impulse buying to a minimum.

MR SPOCK *(Star Trek):*

"May I point out that I had an opportunity to observe your counterparts quite closely. They were brutal, savage, unprincipled, uncivilised, treacherous, in every way, splendid examples of homo sapiens. The very flower of humanity. I found them quite refreshing."

CAPTAIN KIRK *(to Dr McCoy):*

"I'm not sure, but I think we've just been insulted."

"Money doesn't always bring happiness. People with 10 million dollars are no happier than people with 9 million dollars.

HOBART BROWN

The Things to **Remember**

Get your debt working for you - Used carefully and in a methodical way it can work for you as well as against you but don't fall for the lure of consumer cocaine and don't go too far. Balance is key.

Don't leave it too late to start planning - Even if you don't use a financial planner; do something, anything! Save 10% of your income for at least 25 to 30 years. If you have less time, save more. Buy an investment property – anything but DO SOMETHING!

Beware of fear - It stalks you at every turn, trying to get you to go back to old behaviours but there are methods of dealing with it.

Stop when you have enough - Possibly the greatest sin of all, not stopping when you have enough. Plan for all that spare time and don't underestimate the emotional impact of stopping work. You have time to pass on your skills, revive old skills and give something back.

Think about whether any of these apply to you. Imagine you are lying on your death bed with 24 hours left to live. Did you:

Spend too much time at work

Spend too little time with your family

Spend too little time with your friends

Didn't do all the crazy stuff you wanted to

Spend too much time sweating the small stuff

Spend too much time watching television

Spend too much time commuting to work

Didn't give away as much money as you should/could have

Didn't make a real difference in the world

Weren't true to yourself

Didn't take enough risks

Stayed in situations that made you unhappy

Stayed in relationships that made you unhappy

Stayed in a job you no longer enjoyed way beyond when you should have left

Laughed too little

Didn't do stupid things just for the hell of it

Didn't laugh loud enough or often enough

Cried too often

Were sad too often

Didn't see enough movies

Didn't walk out of enough movies when you found they were dreadful

Didn't marvel at enough sunsets

Didn't see your kids grow up

Didn't speak up enough

Didn't let yourself be happier

Didn't have the courage to express your feelings

Didn't take enough risks

Didn't sell the business when you knew you had enough money to never have to work again

Didn't find out if you could have sold the business and never had to work again

Worried too much about what was "around the corner" or "what might go wrong"

Didn't buy that sports car you really, really wanted

Became ill before you had time to do all the stuff you really wanted to do

Were a slave to the opinion of others

The list goes on and on…

"Yesterday is history,
tomorrow's a mystery,
today is a gift which is why it's
called the present.

ALICE MORSE EARLE

Money at a fundamental level is actually pretty simple stuff if you stick to a few basic principles. The trouble is that there are any number of people and institutions out there who complicate it more than necessary, and then charge you handsomely for the privilege. By complicating it, an unnecessary extra layer of risk and cost is usually introduced.

Note the expensive offices in central London and all over the world, the expensive advertising hoardings, the huge bonuses and then you can start to see where your money (yes, **your** money) goes. Witness recently, scandal after scandal hitting the press concerning banks, tax schemes that go wrong, investments that go wrong, and more. Then there is the stuff going on that you don't see; the stuff that does not hit the press.

Despite this there are plenty of "good guys" out there and there are some cracking financial planners out there who can help - check out **www.unbiased.com**.

> *Tip:* Look for a Chartered firm or individual because the Chartered bit shows that they take it seriously.

Finally, **LIFE IS TOO SHORT** to stress over complicated things. Money should be the servant and not the master; it is a means to an end and not the end in itself. Don't forget to enjoy the now and not the tomorrow.